The Hot or Not Game for Couples:
Sexy and Naughty Conversation Starters to Spice Things Up, Break the Ice, and Explore Kinks and Fantasies (All While Laughing)

By Amber Cole

It's not that your sex life has gotten boring, but it's never bad to spice things up and explore a bit, right?

This book has a simple goal: uncover what lies beneath the surface of your sexual desires and fantasies. You might not even know them! And you certainly might not know those of your partner. So each of these questions is designed to be fun, naughty, and educational in a way you can use in the future.

Let's put it this way. Suppose that you have a kink for being tied up and whipped, but none of your partners has ever shown the slightest bit of interest in it. You feel a bit self-conscious and shy about it yourself, so you've never brought it up either. You don't even know if you'd like it in real life, but you sure like to watch porn with people being tied up and whipped.

You'd just never know. Until this book. This book is like opening Pandora's Box and seeing what treasures lie within.

And there are a couple of ways to play. First, you can just treat it like a normal quiz and ask each other the same question. No skips allowed, and both people must answer. No exceptions. You may also find it necessary to place a time limit on thinking. It's tempting to try to come up with the perfect answer but really, your gut instinct and first thought is probably the *honest* answer. This manner of playing is not so much of a quiz or contest, rather just an educational experience and very straightforward way to discover what people want and like.

Second, you can play this book like a true game or quiz. A question will come up, and you will guess the answer for your partner. If you are correct, you get a point. They will then also get a turn to guess your answer to the same question. If they are correct, they also get a point. Keep track of these points, because whoever ends up with the highest score wins the prize.

What's the prize? Well, that's something for you and your partner to decide! But here's a tip: decide the prize after you've gone through the first forty questions. If you decide on a prize before you start playing, it will be before your horizons have been expanded. Wait until #40 and you might have some more interesting prize possibilities!

Even if you don't decide on a fun prize, you can still enjoy the game and laugh together as you discuss and imagine answers and new interests and fantasies. Just focus on fun and the rest will follow. This is a win-win game.

ONE

On top or on bottom? Behind or facing each other? What are your top 3 favorite sex positions?

TWO

Slow and sensual jazz, elevator music, or intense death metal? What kind of music gets you going the most during sex?

THREE

Dominate or submit? Take orders or be in charge? Do you prefer to be the leader or the follower?

FOUR

Sensual massage with fragrant oils and a happy ending (hands only): hot or not?

FIVE

Being recorded and photographed during sex: hot or not? Bonus: watching the videos and pictures together later: hot or not?

SIX

Sex in front of mirrors: hot or not?

SEVEN

Sex in front of an open window, or place you can be observed or watched: hot or not?

EIGHT

A happy wakeup call! Being woken up with oral or sex: hot or not?

NINE

Playing solo or playing with a friend. Masturbating in front of your partner or together mutually: hot or not?

TEN

Grooming as a group activity. Shaving me, shaving you, or shaving each other: hot or not?

ELEVEN

Watching porn together, playing it in the background, or following along with a scene in real life: hot or not?

TWELVE

Make me blush by talking dirty and filthy: hot or not?

THIRTEEN

Give me some of that war paint! Sex on a period: hot or not?

FOURTEEN

It hurts so good. Rough sex to the point of pain and bruising, or just a good round of hair-pulling, spanking, and biting: hot or not?

FIFTEEN

Face sitting: hot or not?

SIXTEEN

Use sex toys on each other or in front of each other: hot or not?

SEVENTEEN

Roleplaying rape (violent or gentle): hot or not?

EIGHTEEN

Choking and slapping: hot or not?

NINETEEN

A finger, a tongue, or a dildo in the ass: hot or not?

TWENTY

Sex in a public and risky area, like a car, public bathroom, or dressing room: hot or not?

TWENTY-ONE

Threesome with two people of the opposite sex or a male and a female: hot or not?

TWENTY-TWO

Couple swapping, swinging, and sex parties: hot or not?

TWENTY-THREE

Make it rain! Strip clubs and lap dances and VIP rooms: hot or not?

TWENTY-FOUR

Have sex with someone else in the room watching: hot or not?

TWENTY-FIVE

Participate in a double penetration: hot or not?

TWENTY-SIX

Feet in or around the genitalia or mouth: hot or not?

TWENTY-SEVEN

Receiving or giving a golden shower: hot or not?

TWENTY-EIGHT

Facials and swallowing: hot or not?

TWENTY-NINE

Nipple clamps and butt plugs: hot or not?

THIRTY

Blindfolds and earplugs: hot or not?

THIRTY-ONE

Drunk or high sex: hot or not?

THIRTY-TWO

Skinny-dipping, streaking, and other kinds of public nudity and exhibitionism: hot or not?

THIRTY-THREE

Hickeys, claw marks, and other sex battle wounds: hot or not?

THIRTY-FOUR

Two birds in one stone. Food and sex: hot or not?

THIRTY-FIVE

Reading erotic stories and novels together: hot or not?

THIRTY-SIX

Leather props, clothing, boots, and texture: hot or not?

THIRTY-SEVEN

Sex in the shower and sex in the Jacuzzi: hot or not?

THIRTY-EIGHT

Dressing up in outfits, like a nurse or fireman: hot or not?

THIRTY-NINE

From gentle to hard. Sucking on the nipples to pinching them: hot or not?

FORTY

69 whether on top or bottom: hot or not?

FORTY-ONE

Roleplay as student and professor, or another kind of power dynamic: hot or not?

FORTY-TWO

Be in the same room as another couple having sex: hot or not?

FORTY-THREE

Being called "daddy" or "mommy" or "baby boy/girl" during sex or otherwise: hot or not?

FORTY-FOUR

Watching or hearing about your partner having sex with someone else: hot or not?

FORTY-FIVE

Gagging and choking during oral: hot or not?

FORTY-SIX

Ropes, knots, Shibari, bondage: hot or not?

FORTY-SEVEN

Edging (being brought to the brink of orgasm and then back) by yourself or by your partner: hot or not?

FORTY-EIGHT

Inflicting or receiving real pain, whether to genitalia or other body parts: hot or not?

FORTY-NINE

Being told when you can and cannot orgasm: hot or not?

FIFTY

Older is better. Sex with a panther, cougar, MILF, DILF, GILF, and so on: hot or not?

FIFTY-ONE

Genital piercings: hot or not?

FIFTY-TWO

Wearing underwear of the opposite sex: hot or not?

FIFTY-THREE

Japanese hentai or other types of cartoon porn: hot or not?

FIFTY-FOUR

Orgies: hot or not?

FIFTY-FIVE

Being the teacher or being the student in bed: which is hotter?

FIFTY-SIX

Sex swings, ramps, restraints, and other equipment: hot or not?

FIFTY-SEVEN

Having a threesome as the third with a couple: hot or not?

FIFTY-EIGHT

Straps, lace and heels or simply nude: which is hotter?

FIFTY-NINE

Swallowing: hot or not?

SIXTY

Having sex in the back of a movie theater: hot or not?

SIXTY-ONE

Huge bush or freshly shaved or waxed: which is hotter?

SIXTY-TWO

5-10 minutes, 10-15 minutes, 15-20 minutes, or longer: which is the best length for sex?

SIXTY-THREE

What kind of underwear do you feel sexiest in?

SIXTY-FOUR

Date night: what should I wear for you?

SIXTY-FIVE

What is your favorite porn genre?

SIXTY-SIX

Cuddling without sex, or sex without cuddling: which is better?

SIXTY-SEVEN

Orgasming through hands, genitalia, or tongue: which is hotter?

SIXTY-EIGHT

5 minutes of foreplay with 20 minutes or sex, or 20 minutes of foreplay with 5 minutes of sex: which is hotter?

SIXTY-NINE

Quickies (under 5 minutes total including penetration and foreplay): hot or not?

SEVENTY

Using vibrators, dildos, and cock rings during sex: hot or not?

SEVENTY-ONE

Being tied down, blindfolded, and teased lightly with a feather: hot or not?

SEVENTY-TWO

Standing sex, against a wall, being carried or carrying: hot or not?

SEVENTY-THREE

Hot sex without orgasms or mediocre sex with an orgasm: which is hotter?

SEVENTY-FOUR

Visiting a sex shop together and picking out clothes and toys: hot or not?

SEVENTY-FIVE

Visiting a professional dominatrix (or being one): hot or not?

SEVENTY-SIX

Giving or receiving road head (oral sex while driving): hot or not?

SEVENTY-SEVEN

Trying to figure out the Kama Sutra together: hot or not?

SEVENTY-EIGHT

Pretending one of you is sleeping while your partner initiates and has sex with you: hot or not? (Or one of you is *actually* sleeping and *not* pretending...)

SEVENTY-NINE

Having sex while staying as silent as possible so as not to get caught or noticed: hot or not?

EIGHTY

Being serviced by your partner like you are at an erotic masseuse, complete with shower and massage, or actually going to an erotic massage together: hot or not?

EIGHTY-ONE

Lube party! Put down an old bedsheet and douse both of you in lube for some slippery fun: hot or not?

EIGHTY-TWO

Feeling helpless or at the mercy of someone's commands: hot or not?

EIGHTY-THREE

Sending or receiving a video of me masturbating for you: hot or not?

EIGHTY-FOUR

Sex while fully clothed: hot or not?

EIGHTY-FIVE

Sex on sexual enhancements like Viagra (for men or women): hot or not?

EIGHTY-SIX

A remote-controlled vibrator for use in public: hot or not?

EIGHTY-SEVEN

Anal beads, double-headed dildos, prostate massagers, and fleshlights: hot or not?

EIGHTY-EIGHT

Swallowing cum, playing with it, spreading it over a body: hot or not?

EIGHTY-NINE

Competing to see who can orgasm first, or who can hold off their orgasm the longest: hot or not?

NINETY

Hold, or have your arms held down or behind your back: hot or not?

NINETY-ONE

Being spit on, spitting on your partner, and being treated disrespectfully: hot or not?

NINETY-TWO

Wearing a short skirt with no panties, or a transparent shirt with no bra (or having your partner dress like that): hot or not?

NINETY-THREE

Put a finger in his ass while he is receiving a blow job: hot or not?

NINETY-FOUR

Cum in her mouth and then make out after: hot or not?

NINETY-FIVE

Squirting and soaking the bed: hot or not?

NINETY-SIX

Only oral, nothing else: hot or not?

NINETY-SEVEN

Outercourse such as titfucking: hot or not?

NINETY-EIGHT

Wrestling and horsing around that leads to sex: hot or not?

NINETY-NINE

Polyamory: hot or not?

ONE HUNDRED

More to love—plus-sized bodies: hot or not?

ONE HUNDRED AND ONE

Taking a sex workshop or class together: hot or not?

ONE HUNDRED AND TWO

Renting a hotel room and pretending to meet downstairs in the hotel lobby: hot or not?

# ONE HUNDRED AND THREE

Role reversal: dominant becomes submissive, and submissive becomes dominant: hot or not?

ONE HUNDRED AND FOUR

Scene reversal: start with sex, then oral, then foreplay: hot or not?

ONE HUNDRED AND FIVE

Slow and tender or fast and hard? Which is hotter, and when and why?

ONE HUNDRED AND SIX

Posting pictures online of you masturbating or having sex for the world to see: hot or not?

ONE HUNDRED AND SEVEN

Ball and gags, cock and ball torture, nipple clamps, electric shocks: hot or not?

www.ingramcontent.com/pod-product-compliance
Lightning Source LLC
Chambersburg PA
CBHW071359080526
44587CB00017B/3137